Quick Gui... Managers

Quick Guide #2

Thinking
Into The Corners™

Michel Theriault

WoodStone Press
Toronto, Canada

I0060010

First Print Edition - ISBN 978-0-9813374-8-7

eBook versions are also available

Published 2014 by WoodStone Press

This book is part of the Quick Guides for Managers series. For information on other related books in the series, visit:

http://www.successfuelformanagers.com/quick-guides/

Summary Contents

"We cannot solve our problems with the same thinking we used when we created them." – Albert Einstein

Table of Contents

Introduction

Thinking Outside The Box is one of those expressions that's attained "cliché status" by virtue of the fact that people think it must be true— simply because it's repeated so frequently.

While there's nothing wrong with trying to think more creatively, I would argue that thinking outside the box can waste a lot of time and energy by encouraging us to focus on ideas and solutions that simply are not feasible.

That's not a productive use of resources. Worse yet, it can demoralize individuals who come up with ideas that can't be implemented.

So the answer isn't about thinking outside the box.

What you really must learn to do involves stretching your thinking to find solutions and ideas that are *within* personal, professional and organizational constraints, yet deliver truly creative (and sometimes even inspirational!) results.

This book and the concept of *Thinking Into The Corners*™ will help ground your thinking in that direction.

As I've seen how this approach can be a catalyst for great ideas and innovative solutions, I'm hopeful it can inspire your own work and workplace.

Michel Theriault

Using This Book

Part 1 - Foundations

This section explains the concept of *Thinking Into The Corners*™ and provides a step-by-step process you can use to implement this approach to get the best possible results from your team during brainstorming or idea-generating sessions.

Part 2 - Methods

Moving on from your new understanding of the process, Part 2 gives you the tools and techniques you need to apply the *Thinking Into The Corners*™ concept to your own problems.

Part 2 starts by addressing the individual or personal limits (which we will define as "circle" limits) that must be overcome to develop ideas and solutions more effectively. It also addresses ways to reduce any negative impact from those limits, such as change-adverse "push back" that can prevent people from stretching into the corners or suppress the open exchange of ideas during group sessions.

Some of the most common tools for generating ideas are also discussed in Part 2. While some of the tools will be familiar to readers, the way you use these tools is what matters when it comes to applying tried and true tools to your *Thinking Into The Corners*™ process.

Part 1 - Foundations

While management consultants and business leaders everywhere have been telling us to think outside the box since the 1970s, that expression can be a barrier to generating effective ideas and solutions.

> *"If everyone has to think outside the box,*
> *maybe it is the box that needs fixing."*
> *~Malcolm Gladwell*

The techniques we use to develop ideas are not the problem.

Nor is it wrong to view innovation as good. But it is problematic to assume that you and your staff have to come up with ideas that are so far out there that nobody's considered them before.

If we're being honest, there's often a good reason we do the things we do, personally and organizationally. (Round wheels work precisely because they're round.)

But if the principles of creative thinking are positive and the techniques we use to draw out new ideas and principles are still sound, where's the problem? Perhaps the issue is with the way we frame the quest for innovation.

Instead of thinking outside the box, it's time we set practical, limited and realistic boundaries.

This approach ensures you and your staff spend time and energy developing ideas and solutions that can be implemented.

Working within defined limits (a.k.a.: the box) also gives us an opportunity to test those limits—and set new boundaries.

That's right. Instead of merely recognizing the barriers, we push them. The creative act of setting new boundaries thus begins with an honest look at what's possible right now and then using that to discover what's possible in the future.

Staying Inside The Box

We all have boxes we must stay
within, why not embrace the
constraints?

> *"We're always told to think outside the box.*
> *But it's about time someone spoke up for the*
> *box. Because, paradoxically, thinking inside*
> *a box can spark creativity, not squelch it."*
> *- Dan Heath and Chip Heath*

One of the biggest challenges managers face involves the push to develop new great ideas. "Think outside the box" is a common rallying call to those who are supposed to generate creativity and advance new ideas.

Unfortunately, access to such a wide open canvas actually makes it hard for participants to develop concrete, useable and implementable ideas. It also misses an important point: we all have limits that constrict our options and our ideas.

Advocates of thinking outside the box may think it's counterintuitive to establish a framework for discussions about innovation. In reality, establishing the framework (defining limits to the box) makes you and your staff better equipped to think about solutions.

Instead of wasting time and energy on issues outside of the box, this approach frees you to focus on solutions that are within reach—as long as you give yourself and your workforce the encouragement to extend your reach.

That's the concept of *Thinking Into The Corners*™.

The basic principle of this approach is incredibly simple. When you have a box to work with, you have a quantifiable, defined work area. As soon as you say you need to think outside the box, your work area becomes infinite, undetermined—and daunting.

While you may use that space and time to think up lots of creative ideas, most of them will be completely unworkable. Many may not even be related to the issue or problem at hand.

Some the best ideas are formed by a catalyst. The catalyst itself might not be readily obvious or predictable. But once it reveals itself, the catalyst is likely to be rooted in a concrete, well-defined concept that wasn't even necessarily "way out there."

Think about it this way. If you were given a blank sheet of paper and simply told to write something down, you would spend valuable time trying to figure out what to write and how what you write may or may not be useful. Indeed, most of us would even wonder *why* we were asked to do this particular task.

Now imagine your response if same sheet of paper included printed guidelines, possible topics and noted subjects you should not write about. The latter approach makes it much more likely that you will quickly settle on something to write about. What you write is also apt to be more relevant.

While some of this is about defining the goals and objectives of the thinking process, it's hard to do that without first setting finite limits.

In essence, this approach means you start by defining the box and therefore, your limits. That means you aren't really thinking outside the box. The sooner you admit it, the better.

Next, you examine those limits closely to see whether they can be stretched. This isn't "blue sky" thinking, it's a practical approach to finding a solution that can work.

This frees you and your team to stop believing true creativity comes from some other-worldly place fuelled by creative Zen. Now you can develop ideas that actually achieve your goals and objectives within existing boundaries, regardless of whether your quest is for a new business idea, product, process or a solution to a problem.

Instead of being paralyzed by the wide open space surrounding your box, start to think about what is inside the box—and what might be in the corners.

Thinking Into The Corners™

Successfully developing and fostering ideas from your team improves your success.

"We are addicted to our thoughts. We cannot change anything if we cannot change our thinking." ~ Santosh Kalway

By removing the unlimited and paralyzing space outside the box, *Thinking Into The Corners*™ helps you develop the kind of "thinking within limits" that actually provide a catalyst for innovation.

Instead of seeing the box as confining, proponents of this approach recognize the external limits. This gives us a place from which we can methodically challenge and then test those limits. The end result is a bigger box, since pushing the limits serves to expand the box and give us access to solutions lurking in the corners.

But what about the internal limits that act as a kind of circle inside the box? As is evident in the diagram that follows, the reality of the circle inside the box is that it sets other limits that keep us from "stretching" into the corners.

This illustration shows how the box and the circle interact— and how this interaction can prevent us from discovering the untapped opportunity that exist in the corners of our box.

The bottom line is that if you put all of your energy into thinking outside the box, you miss the untapped opportunity found in the corners. But because our thinking is often constrained by our own self limits (our "circles"), we tend to miss solutions inside our own box—and waste resources on outside-the-box solutions that we can't achieve.

In fact, the real opportunities are when you stretch yourself and your team to think into the corners.

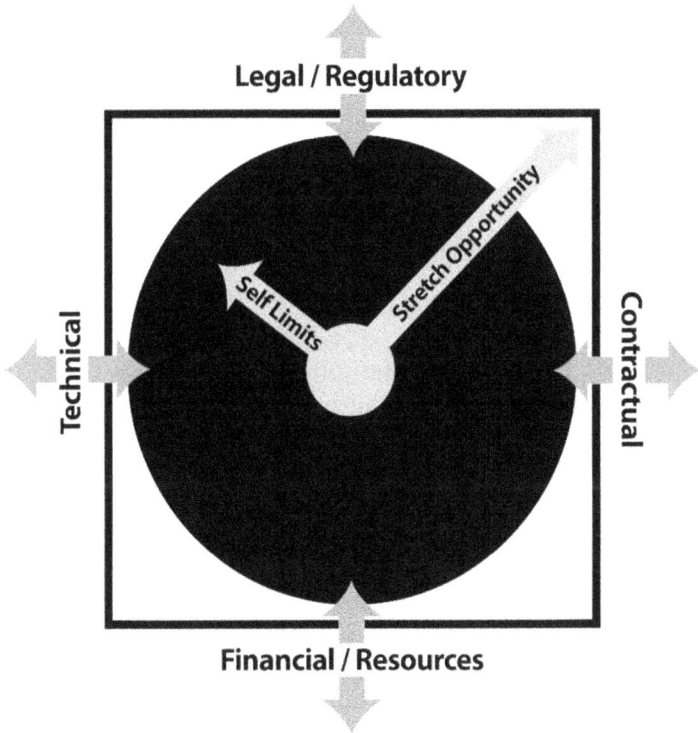

Like all good concepts, *Thinking Into The Corners*™ isn't difficult; it simply sets the stage to get the best results from your team.

Thinking Into The Corners™ is the opposite of the old notion that you have to "think outside the box" to generate ideas and solutions. That said, it does rely on techniques often associated with "outside the box" strategies, including group discussion, problem solving and idea generation—all of which are critical to innovation.

Since we all have limitations (boxes) we can't go outside of, let's focus on solutions that are within those limitations.

In fact, creativity within a framework is more effective for most of us, while abstract thinking is not a good way to get results.

After all, great thinking isn't necessarily about simply being creative; it's about being creative in achieving your desired results.

Consider This

If you give someone a coloring book with a picture of a cat and tell them they can color outside the lines, you may end up with a rabbit. That's ok, unless you really need a picture of a cat.

The reality is that there are always limits we simply can't do anything about. But spending time on ideas that can't be implemented is a waste of time and demoralizing to your team.

What we need are practical, achievable ideas. The ideas we find can look very creative—but most will come from inside the box.

The Box

The parameters of the box we have to work within has always been seen as a limit to overcome, particularly for those determined to explore the think-outside-the-box philosophy.

As noted earlier, however, when it comes to thinking and idea generation, it makes more sense to define the sides of the box as a framework and catalyst (versus a limitation).

Since we all truly have a box in which we have to operate, it makes sense to define the outer limits of the box and then anchor our creative process around those limits. This keeps us from wasting time on a process that leads us well beyond where we need to be, or in fact are able to go.

If you're tasked with finding new ideas to old problems, the box gives you the outside limits to use in your solution. By recognizing those limits and even closely testing and examining them, you're likely to find solutions you didn't know exist.

Study the following illustration. While you may identify other limits to consider in addition to these four, they are a good place to begin this process.

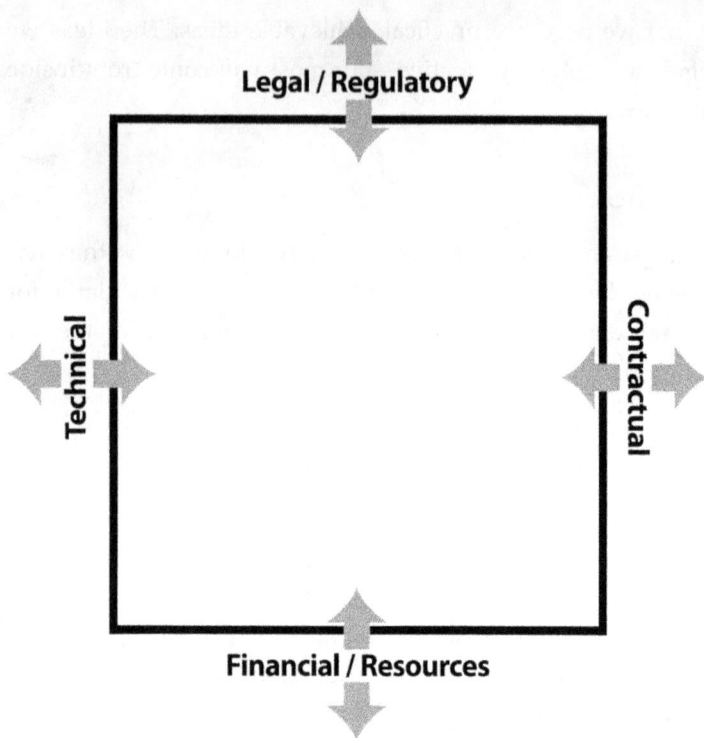

Legal / Regulatory

Technical

Contractual

Financial / Resources

Legal / Regulatory Limits

The law, including regulations that you, your company or your product or service have to follow, typically set a fairly rigid limit. Among other details, they may govern what you can and can't claim about your product, how it's packaged and the products, procedures and materials you can and can't use.

While these are clearly defined limits, careful examination of those limits can sometimes identify opportunities you didn't realize were there. Again, you are not ignoring the limits, but working within them.

Contractual Limits

By their nature, contracts impose limits on what we do. Unlike other limits, however, contractual limits are usually agreed upon through negotiations. Sometimes, they are a trade-off to remove other limits.

What makes contractual limits important to this discussion is the fact that contracts can be re-interpreted, re-negotiated—and even changed.

Working with the contractual limits, instead of trying to ignore them when coming up with new, creative ideas, is more likely to result in changes that can be done instead of those that are hopeful—but unlikely.

Technical Limits

These kinds of limits can range from the laws of nature (which can't be changed) to technical limits that might be expanded with the right investment and study. Scientific progress is paved with change, after all.

Again, rather than simply ignoring technical limits, acknowledge them and look closely for opportunities to expand the technical box.

This ensures that even if you can't supersede technical limits, you will fully understand those limits and be better able to find solutions that adhere to those limits. This is far better than trying to find solutions that ignore the reality of technical limits! Those who chase the impossible often have to work backwards after a failed and time-consuming attempt to make an unworkable idea work.

Financial / Resource Limits

These limits are probably the most flexible. Since financial and resource limits may be influenced by the ideas themselves, organizations might justify increasing this limit if the ideas/arguments are good enough.

But not every new idea deserves extra money to make it happen. When you are considering ideas, the financial and resource limits you have to work within must be considered first. Where possible, solutions and ideas should also fit inside the current box.

That may include re-allocating money and people, for instance, or putting another project or initiative on hold until you can implement your new ones and prove them they work. Recognizing the limits and working within them is how you can think into the corners.

One caveat: if your ideas and solutions are workable given the legal/regulatory, contractual and technical limits, the financial/resource area may be able to stretch to accommodate innovation. But expanding this side of the box should never be a starting point, even when the other parameters are met. Again, working within the box is a better option.

Unlike the circle limits we will discuss next (which are more specific to the person and the organization), those working in similar situations could arguably be said to have the same sized box.

While different individuals in comparable situations may be able to change the size of their boxes, your challenge when developing creative ideas is first to make sure the box you're working with is as large as possible. That demands a critical look at the box's real boundaries. Appropriate, realistic and well understood limits on the creative process come from knowing what you've really got to work with.

For instance, while contractual limits are part of the box, there may be clauses built into those contracts that let you expand that part of the box. Unless you stretch your thinking to examine these limits—and then explore ways to use them to your advantage—you may not find the best solutions.

Consider This

Thinking Into The Corners™ is flexible. As you are able to expand your box, your circle also needs to expand, enabling you to reach the corners where the best ideas are found.

When you start the process of expanding your circle and reaching into the corners of the box, you have to communicate the limits as you know them to the participants taking part in the idea- and solution-generation process.

The Circle

Once you understand how to define—and expand—the box limits, you need to realize how the "circle" works within the box. This is essential because it will help you and your staff break out of the self-limitations that exist when developing new ideas.

In a nutshell, circle limits affect you and your staff's ability to create new products, develop processes, create strategic plans, solve problems and even recognize issues and problems in the first place.

While one can argue that our own self-limits keep most of us within a safe, comfortable range, it's important to recognize that comfort also keeps most of us from stretching to find new ideas to implement. Why stretch when the status quo is so easy?

Worse yet, filters can have a compounded impact. Facilitators leading group efforts to generate innovative ideas must be aware of this potential.

Consider This

Recognizing limits and knowing how to mitigate this filter is the first step to better thinking.

The limits imposed by filters result from a combination of many different factors, including our personal influences. Think about it: even though we all have different-sized professional and social circles, we influence—and are influenced by—others.

While the limitations imposed by the circle can be obvious, they are usually subtle. Because the most subtle of these limits are based on our own backgrounds, personal situations, comfort levels, motivations and even the environment where the ideas and thinking take place, we may not even know when the limits are at work.

To optimize the idea-generating strategies employed by *Thinking Into The Corners*™, it's important to recognize the main categories of limitations, or filters. The filters listed below are expanded in Part 2 – Methods, where details about how to counter their negative impact are also presented.

- ✓ **Sunglasses** – This filter is usually the result of experience and background.
- ✓ **Time / Effort** –This filter is a result of extra effort or time an idea may take.
- ✓ **Group think** – This filter is the result of a group environment.

- ✓ **Deferral** – This filter shows itself when it's easy to defer decision or action.
- ✓ **Risk Aversion** – This filter is applied when there is the possibility of failure.

Personality-related filters also impact the overall idea-generation process (such as brainstorming). Because they often appear to be inflexible, personality-related filters can impact other participants during the brainstorming sessions. These are also expanded in Part 2 – Methods.

- ✓ **Dominator –** When one person is dominant and forceful, it may limit ideas from those who are intimidated.
- ✓ **The Authority –** When someone with authority over others contributes, they may dampen other opinions because of the impact of hierarchy.
- ✓ **Expert –** Individuals are sometimes seen as the expert in an area and others defer to their opinions— regardless of whether they are right or not.
- ✓ **Saboteur –** This filter happens when someone intentionally sabotages the process and ideas for their own reasons.
- ✓ **Wallflower –** This is when participants don't contribute their ideas, either because they lack confidence, are uncertain, or defer to other dominant participants.

Quick Summary

Key Points

➡ Don't try to think outside the box—boundaries help your creative process.

➡ Everyone's box includes a circle created by filters that may suppress the best ideas.

➡ You have to put the conditions in place for the best collaboration and teamwork.

Executive Tips

➡ Many existing tools can be used to help you generate ideas and solutions with your team.

➡ Recognize the filters and work to counteract them.

Traps to Avoid

➡ Don't use the "blue-sky" approach to idea generation, it may waste time generating impractical ideas

➡ Don't make groups from all the same people and experiences. Mixing it up will give you better results.

Your Plan

Based on what you've read, what will you do to develop creative ideas and solutions to improve results?

What are you going to do?	When

Notes

_____

_____

_____

_____

_____

_____

_____

_____

_____

_____

_____

_____

Stretching Into The Corners

Successfully developing and fostering
ideas from your team improves your
success.

> *"People don't like to think. If one thinks, one
> must reach conclusions. Conclusions are not
> always pleasant." – Helen Keller*

Building on what's been discussed so far, it's evident that to develop creative solutions, you and your team need to stretch your thinking into the corners of the box and move outside your circle limits.

Keep in mind that when we talk about team solutions, many of the concepts we address can be applied to individual problem solving, too.

This important part of the process is about setting up your creative problem-solving exercise based on the box and circle so you can generate practical solutions and ideas that you can implement. It is in direct contrast to a process that would have developed ideas that don't have any hope of succeeding because they are "outside the box."

By setting up the environment first, based on the principles of *Thinking Into The Corners*™, you will get much more value out of the existing range of techniques and tools for generating ideas. Many of them are listed and discussed in Part 2—

Methods, along with suggestions on how to make them work best for *Thinking Into The Corners*™.

The process is mostly about communicating and understanding the limits of your box (and expanding the box based on that understanding). This allows you and your team to be focused and productive while also identifying and eliminating the things that create the circles that limit the reach of individuals involved.

Consider This

Like a search and rescue operation, limiting the area of the search based on known information makes it easier to find the solution you are looking for.

The following outlines the steps for using *Thinking Into The Corners*™ for problem solving and idea generation. Once you understand the steps, you can use the tools and techniques in the next section to work with your team to develop those ideas using well-established techniques adapted for *Thinking Into The Corners*™.

Step 1 - Establish The Problem

The first limits you establish have to do with the problem itself. Without it, you might as well be throwing darts to find a solution. It is, however, critical to define the problem effectively so you and your team can better develop solutions and ideas that work.

What To Do

Develop a clear, concise statement about what the problem is and any parameters that need to be considered.

Make sure you put it into a context that the participants in your problem-solving session can understand. Recognize that you may have to adapt the problem, or describe it so a wide range of people will understand it, depending on the make-up of your team. If you have finance people mixed with technical production people, for instance, you will need to define the problem in ways that both groups are likely to understand.

Having a diverse team working on your problem is a good thing, so spend the effort on defining the problem for them instead of assembling a team of like-minded individuals.

How To Do It

Depending on the nature of your problem, you will have to frame the problem based on the root cause or on the ultimate outcome you expect. Sometimes, the problem needs both frames.

It's critical to identify the root cause or reason you need to solve the problem. This information helps your staff frame the issue and makes it easier for them to come up with solutions.

Consider This

This is the same principle as the "command intent" principle used in the military. Under command intent, the reason for achieving an objective is outlined along the command and an objective. This increases the likelihood of achieving the goal.

If necessary, use a root cause analysis process with a fishbone diagram (as described below) to identify the real problem you need to deal with. There may be more than one cause, of course.

Framing the problem can be very similar to developing a mission statement, with a few more details added in to give enough context and enable effective solution building.

This quote, part of President J.F. Kennedy's speech about the goal to reach the moon, provides details that would be useful in framing the problem and developing the solution:

"... we shall send to the moon, 240,000 miles away from the control station in Houston, a giant rocket more than 300 feet tall, the length of this football field, made of new metal alloys, some of which have not yet been invented, capable of standing heat and stresses several times more than have ever been experienced, fitted together with a precision better than the finest watch, carrying all the equipment needed for propulsion, guidance, control, communications, food and survival, on an untried mission, to an unknown celestial body, and then return it safely to earth, re-entering the atmosphere at speeds of over 25,000 miles per hour, causing heat about half that of the temperature of the sun..."

Clearly, some of the parameters (the box) had already been established and he used those in his speech as part of framing the problem.

Consider This

While this seems to provide limits on what the solution might ultimately look like, without the parameters, the solution would be harder to find.

You can develop these parameters independently or, for best results, include a process to establish them in the first part of your group problem-solving session. Getting your team to help firm up your problem can benefit the subsequent processes, unless the problem or objective is so clear that this part of the group process isn't needed.

Regardless of your process for Step 1, the subsequent steps are all done with the full team involvement in a formal session or in several sessions.

Step 2 - Identifying Box Limits

This step is necessary before you think about the next step, expanding the box limits.

It can be fun for participants, since they can challenge or chip away at what are perceived limits to arrive at the real limits. That positions the team to expand the limits when they tackle the second part of the process.

What to Do

Once you have defined the problem, you can then frame your limits around them using the sides of the box.

Consider This

It is possible you will have other limits that also need to be defined.

For each of the sides, develop a statement or establish specific limits that provide a reference point for participants in the subsequent step.

Like the overall approach to providing limits that help develop ideas, providing your thoughts on the limits or even a starting list will be a catalyst for your group to participate with a full understanding of the concept.

These are the four sides of the Box.

➡ Legal/regulatory

➡ Contractual

➡ Technical

➡ Financial / Resources

How To Do It

Starting with your statement or your initial list, get each participant to contribute their understanding of the limits. You can do this using traditional brainstorming techniques you are comfortable with.

Depending on your group dynamics, have them participate orally or get them to write the limits on paper and hand them in for general discussion.

Pad board the limits, combining similar ones. Get agreement about the limits at this point and discuss why they are limits.

These become your initial box limits.

Step 3 - Expanding The Box

This is a key part of the concept. After you've completed Step 2, take the limits you defined and explore each of the limits to see if you can expand those limits from a realistic and practical perspective. Keep in mind that expanded limits can sometimes only apply going forward and not to current issues or contracts. (But that's fine. It's good to know where the box limits stand and how they can be expanded in the future.)

What To Do

In this step, you examine and probe each limit to fully understand the limits you identified and find out whether you can expand those limits—and your box.

While the intent isn't to find solutions or creative ideas, sometimes the process of looking at expanding the limits in itself will generate ideas that are "into the corners." That's a happy by-product of the process. Be sure to write these ideas down and park them for later use. Don't let them derail the current step, but don't risk losing them either.

How To Do It

Don't just do this superficially; probe and explore each limit aggressively.

Ask why the limit is there and why it can't be expanded. Then ask more questions until you exhaust all avenues and opportunities.

This is where the participation of a multi-functional group is especially important, since new or different perspectives can provide insight that an expert oversees. But carefully consider the limits or filters, including those related to personalities, that can negatively impact the process of developing solutions.

For instance, instead of only asking the lawyers to look at the contractual and legal issues, the operations folks to look at the technical limits, your finance folks to look at financial limits, etc., work it through the process as a team with a variety of participants.

Consider This

Sometimes subject matter experts have a hard time seeing options for expanding the box themselves.

In addition to generating ideas or solutions by virtue of the cross-pollination of input from various sources, a diverse group is better able to create the new boundaries that will act as limits—and catalysts—for subsequent steps. The key is to ask the right questions.

Legal / Regulatory

This is where interpretation can influence your box. Look at the regulation section by section and fully understand not only what's said, but also the intent and what's not said. A careful approach can identify legal/regulatory issues, perhaps buried within clauses that you hadn't even considered in the past.

Where possible, look to precedent, whether in legal cases or regulatory findings, to find out how flexible the regulations actually are.

Contractual

While contracts are often seen as fixed, opportunities for renegotiation abound. Even if you can't change what's in a current contract, you can find information you can use to change future ones. This may be where you can expand your box.

Review all the relevant contract clauses to find opportunities, interpretations or even gaps. You may find items you can change without negotiation, as well as items that will require negotiation with the other party to make work.

Never assume you can't make changes. You may need to have a compelling reason for the change, but that compelling reason may be apparent in the solution proposed.

Technical

There are often different solutions or work-arounds to technical issues. Unfortunately, our filters can prevent their identification. Lifting those filters may have a positive—and powerful—impact on how we understand the parameters of our box.

This is where technical experts can help, but some of the best input may come from experts not invested in the current situation. These individuals may not have the same filters as people on the inside. This lets them see where limits can be stretched and solutions can be found.

Financial / Resources

While every organization has financial/resources limits, creativity can sometimes expand this side of the box. The solution may come from diverting resources from somewhere else or from sourcing funds and resources differently.

Knowing how you can expand this box (even through fund/resource diversion) broadens the potential to find creative solutions through the application of new ideas. The solutions themselves may make the case for increased financial resources, so don't hold back. If you can make the case, do it.

Step 4 - Stretching Into The Corners

Now that you've defined and expanded the box as much as you can and have started to explore creative ideas, you can apply solutions based on what you've learned from examining your limits. The next step is to find ideas that stretch into the corners. These solutions will be creative and new, but will also work within your newly-established (and expanded) constraints.

To be clear: you are still working inside the box, but certain sides of that box may have expanded.

What To Do

At this stage, the process of generating ideas is similar to what you have probably used before, such as brainstorming. But your starting point has shifted. You begin the next step in your process with defined box limits and a better understanding of your team's circle limits.

That's right. By defining the limits of your box you are now ready to apply the critical principles of *Thinking Into The Corners*™. Using these principles as a basis for creative ideas and understanding (and getting around) the participant's self-limits, you open the doors that might limit creative (yet realistic) problem solving and idea generation.

Those self-limits, along with techniques to defeat them, are discussed in Part 2—Methods. That section also addresses the problem-solving tools you can use to develop ideas.

While each of these methods has its advantages and disadvantages, they are all useful. Of course, you may even want to use more than one with your team.

How To Do It

Conduct your problem solving in a structured, well-managed session that focuses on the problem and the need for a collaborative and concrete result that can be actioned.

Consider This

If you are part of the team and your contribution is important, you shouldn't facilitate the session. Instead, get someone else to do it. The facilitator should understand the process and the requirements, but they are there to facilitate, not as a subject matter expert. A facilitator helps manage individual contributions, focus the discussion, cut-off tangential discussion, deal with filters and otherwise guide the team towards its goals.

Even though the tools in Part 2—Methods are probably familiar to you, the first three steps you did to prepare and then managing the process of using these tools for *Thinking Into The Corners*™ are very important.

Start by posting on the wall the limits you developed. You want them to be easy to see. Write on pad board paper so the limits are large enough, one for each side of the box. Depending on the limits, you may need additional sheets to capture them all or put them in specific categories for your needs.

Then document ideas using pad boards or whiteboards during the creative process. You can also use extra-large sticky notes for this process.

While the convention for brainstorming is that you don't "red light" ideas as they are produced, for this process you do need to test each idea against the limits. Where ideas go outside of the limits, you can park them for future examination. Don't spend time dealing with them during this process.

If you have a large team and the time, duplicate the exercise with a different group and see whether the results are the same. Try to mix the groups so each has a good representation of individuals and expertise.

Since the group will have different filters, they may see things differently and that's usually a good thing.

If the results aren't consistent, then you should explore why and re-assess. Even getting both teams together and discussing the differences may help with the decision.

Step 5 - Prioritize

Once you have a handful (or more) of viable ideas that are within your box limits, you have to decide which ones merit more time or development.

As you have limited resources to implement ideas, culling the ideas to the ones most likely to work is an important next step.

What To Do

Look closely at each idea, tune them up if necessary with additional assumptions and information and establish the likely benefits and the costs to implement in funding, resources and time.

Prioritize them in order of benefit and viability so you can take the next step.

How To Do It

Start by looking at each idea in more detail. You can do this within your idea session. If you don't have time to do that, take it off-line or convene a group to specifically tackle this stage.

Expand the ideas to ensure you have addressed all the issues. This will also help you prioritize the ideas. This doesn't have to be highly detailed. Do provide enough information to compare and prioritize the options.

Assess the likely value they will bring, the resources they will cost and the risk of implementing them.

Since you probably can't do everything, rank the ideas with the team. This helps you identify ideas with the highest impact, as well as those that will take the least amount of resources or work. Make these your focus.

Use a quadrant assessment like the one described in Part 2—Methods and shown below. Chose the items that appear in the High Value sections and prioritize them based on their placement.

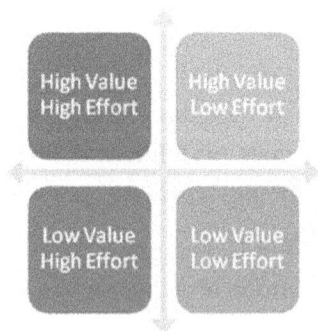

Step 6 - Select & Implement

Once you prioritize the ideas, it's time to select the ones you want to implement.

What To Do

You prioritized your ideas in the last step based on the cost and benefit. Now you want to take another look and decide which to move forward with.

How To Do It

Look at each of the prioritized ideas. Assess them again against less tangible issues such as likelihood of success, politics, resource cost and others.

You may not end up selecting the ones at the top of your priority list. They may give you better benefits, but may come at a cost or risk that you don't want to pursue at this time. Those are legitimate (in-the-box) reasons for starting elsewhere.

It may be better to select an action item with lower effort, or one that has less risk vis-à-vis other issues or politics at work. You may also want to start by tackling an idea you can implement within your responsibilities without having to justify it upwards. A key strategy is to implement an idea with a high likelihood of success. This gives you the credibility to tackle other higher risk (and higher reward) ideas next.

If implementation requires a business case or other justification, be sure to fully document the reasons and assumptions for the decision and use them in your business case.

Once you've selected an idea to proceed with and you've secured necessary approvals, begin your implementation.

Consider This

A successful implementation demonstrates to your team and your boss that the process is valuable and that positive change is possible. With a success under your belt, you can tackle the harder issues.

Key Points	➡	The box isn't an absolute, it can be expanded.
	➡	Traditional idea-generating techniques can be used to think into the corners.
	➡	Prioritizing and implementing ideas that will be successful helps you tackle more difficult solutions.

| **Executive Tips** | ➡ | Sometimes expanding the box reveals ideas you may not otherwise have seen. |
| | ➡ | You shouldn't facilitate the session yourself; it will get in the way of your own contribution and may stifle your team members' contributions. |

Traps to Avoid	➡	Don't let ideas and solutions that can't work sap your team's time and effort.
	➡	When you use the traditional idea-generating techniques like brainstorming, don't revert to the same old approach.
	➡	Don't ever assume a box limit can't be expanded.

Your Plan

Based on what you've read, what will you do to develop creative ideas and solutions to improve results?

What are you going to do?	When

Notes

_____

_____

_____

_____

_____

_____

_____

_____

_____

_____

_____

Part 2 - Methods

Thinking Into The Corners™ isn't merely a more practical alternative to "Thinking Outside The Box."

You need to manage the creative process better to generate creative, useful ideas that stretch you and your team's thinking.

While some of it comes from developing the creative ideas within the defined limits of the box or through carefully examining the box limits and then stretching them, you also need to remove the self-imposed limits created by the circle.

Those circle limits come in the form of filters that most of us have, whether we think we have them or not. These limits are also imposed by the interaction of different personalities acting within the group dynamic of an idea-generation session.

Only by understanding and the breaking down these limits will you be able to effectively stretch into the corners for the ideas and solutions that will let you benefit from this different approach.

This section identifies those limits and provides you with techniques to overcome them.

It also discusses some of the traditional idea-generating techniques and provides ideas about how to apply these tried and true methods to *Thinking Into The Corners*™.

Tackling The Circle

Removing filters that prevent creative
ideas improves your success.

---

*"The conventional view serves to protect us
from the painful job of thinking" ~ John
Kenneth Galbraith*

We all develop filters that affect how we think, create and
function. They are based on our experiences and internal
factors such as our desire to maintain the status quo, keep our
job, stay comfortable and more.

Whether we recognize them or not, these filters act on all of
us every day. We all have them (albeit to varying degrees)
and they all contribute to the size of our circle. They also set
limits that define our comfort zone.

Recognizing the internal or self-imposed limits that affect you
and your team's ability to creatively solve problems and
implement new solutions is an important step to improving
results.

While filters affect us all in different ways, understanding them is essential if you want to eliminate or minimize how they impact your ability to stretch into the corners of your box. If you're serious about getting better results—you've got to get serious about understanding your circle.

If you are facilitating idea and problem-solving sessions, awareness of these filter-imposed-limits will make your process much more effective.

Consider This

You have filters, too. Carefully assess your own situation and the filters that make up your circle limits and deal with them like you would deal with someone else's filters if they were getting in the way of your process. If you are participating, but have a neutral facilitator, they should deal with you—and your filters—the same as anyone else's.

Keep in mind that some of these filters are related to the personalities discussed in a later section.

Identify Limits

Your goal here is to identify the circle limits/filters and be aware of them so you can eliminate as many as possible.

In some cases, you will be aware of the limits and simply use that information to guide the process and contributions. Some filters may need to be removed. The impact of others can be limited by awareness and analysis.

In the latter cases, you will need to make the participants aware of their limits so they can try to remove or manage the limits so as to minimize any negative impact.

You must also recognize your own limits and minimize their impact.

Filter management is best done before you begin a session. You may need to meet with individual members of the group. At the very least, you will need to know what kind of filters they are likely to employ. These may include professional biases related to their work. As mentioned earlier, one way to manage those biases is to work with small groups that represent a cross-section of an organization. You do not, for example, keep all of the technical staff together, or strike a group of all accountants.

By considering the participants and pinpointing their possible filters, you are identifying how these filters may impact your process. And filter issues won't all be related to specific work. You also want to be aware of less obvious filters. Perhaps members feel overworked and fear being given more work to do. Others may be leery of change imposed from "outside." You may also have individuals who simply don't like change.

Once you identify the limits and where possible, have spoken to each of the participants, think about how you can deal with these filters in the facilitated session. You may need to acknowledge the existence of certain filters at the outset, or identify your interest in improving work conditions through efficiencies versus doing-more-with-less.

If possible, you could identify alternate resources you are willing to bring onboard. If it looks like problems with current practices will hold back the discussion and innovation, make a clear statement about launching a process that's about looking forward, not back.

Consider This

You won't be able to completely eliminate each filter, but you can minimize them when you know they exist.

Here are some strategies you can use to deal with some of the most common circle constraints.

Sunglasses

We wear sunglasses because they provide a level of self-protection from the environment and the people who populate it. From an organizational management and change perspective, however, sunglasses act as a filter that keep us from recognizing solutions that are in the corners of the box.

Sunglasses act as an internal (personal) filter. Because they limit our view, they contribute to a reluctance for change that comes from being "set in our ways." In essence, they protect our own status quo—and prevent us from seeing what's really there. Sunglasses help us justify an existing state of affairs.

The end result is a propensity to maintain present circumstances. Sunglasses lead us to make statements like, "that's the way it's always been done" and "we don't try ideas that haven't worked before." This filter lets us hold onto our assumptions. It also prevents us from getting new information. Indeed, sunglasses nurture our own bias towards experts, authorities and even our boss's opinions.

To be clear, this filter's negative impact is not always intentional. Many factors impact our ability to suppress or limit our own thinking and the sunglass filter is simply one way to describe what's going on.

How To Mitigate This Filter

First, you need to recognize the effect in yourself and know that it exists in other participants. It may not always be clear that you or others are wearing sunglasses—but this is a filter you should deliberately identify.

The sunglass filter is often what's behind situations where you hear people agree with a statement that supports the status quo and dismisses alternatives before they can be explored. In sum, sunglasses can block a working group's ability to think deeper about the issue. They also keep groups from identifying roadblocks or coming up with alternatives or improvements.

While the problems caused by sunglass filters are not always intentional, we should acknowledge there are times when intentional harm occurs. If that's the case, structure your idea-generation processes to reduce the discomfort from abandoning our assumptions and using new information

Based on your observations of how this filter might impact individual members of your group—and then spread to others—quietly talk to individuals who you think might be wearing sunglasses. Let them know how this filter works and how it impacts idea generation. People may not realize they are doing it.

Since recognizing this filter is essential to your process, facilitators can also ask questions that challenge participants, as a whole or as individuals, to recognize which sunglasses they should remove. Otherwise, they may simply hide behind them.

What To Do Before The Session

If you've seen this behaviour at work in a group dynamic before, or know of an individual who is likely to wear their sunglasses to a brainstorming session, address the issue up front. That might mean approaching certain members before a group session.

Encourage these individuals to recognize that they are not always seeing the whole landscape. Ergo, they are not contributing to the level they should. Give them examples of how their sunglasses may hold them back.

Then encourage them to take their sunglasses off. You may have to acknowledge and deal with other concerns, including the reason for donning the sunglasses in the first place. These conversations can yield valuable insight into other issues that could also threaten your process. These include personality traits like those addressed in the next section.

What To Do During The Session

There might be times when you don't recognize this filter at work until during the session. If you keep it in mind, you can manage the situation to eliminate the negative impact of the sunglasses.

Sample Situation

You know someone has the experience to contribute and identify issues around a solution, but they aren't contributing during the session.

Action

Ask them a direct question to get their contribution. Say something like, "John, I know you have lots of insight into this. Can you list 3 specific things that have to be done before this solution can work?"

You may need to provoke them. Say, "team, you've given some pretty tame scenarios. Let's crank it up a little and look at the worst case situation. John, I know you had a near-miss, can you start the discussion with that?"

Or challenge them. Say, "John, You've been silent so far, but I know you've had problems in this area before. Based on your experience, what is the most important thing to consider?"

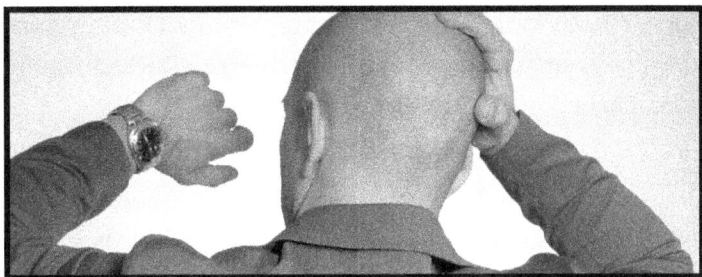

Time/Effort

The time/effort filter often applies when the solution or initiative that may result from the idea will take time and effort to implement. When everyone is already busy (or perceives themselves as busy), it's sometimes easier to stay quiet instead of making suggestions you may have to act on.

This says more about resources and effort than it does about being lazy. More importantly, this filter prevents you and your staff from getting into the corners to identify new ideas and solutions simply because they may require effort to plan and implement.

The external limitations of time/effort aside, we must acknowledge that this filter dampens our creativity. To some extent, we all use this filter to balance our lives. At work, this filter minimizes the risk of failure related to taking on additional tasks that could impact our ability meet production and performance measurements.

Type "A" personalities are often immune since they typically have no problem staying late or working at home to perfect their work.

But for many others, ideas that threaten to take extra time, keep us from our personal lives and families or require additional effort, may never see the light of day.

This filter is at work every time people see something that could be improved, but decide against taking action because they don't want to risk adding more weight to their own workload. While assessing time and effort against benefits is a valid way to prioritize, it's best to formally assess the ideas rather than making assumptions in our minds.

How To Mitigate This Filter

Issues related to the resources needed to act on new ideas must be dealt with up-front. It's easier to come up with ideas if you aren't worried about the time and effort it will take to implement them or make them part of your process.

The best way to deal with this filter is to eliminate it. To do this, you must ensure participants are confident that appropriate resources will be found such that new ideas can be implemented without adding to their current workload. This can include delaying other innovations while the new initiatives are implemented.

One way to mitigate the time/effort impact of change is to ensure the process of finding new ideas includes participants who won't be impacted as their input will be less impacted by the time/effort filter. That said, you still have to deal with those who might be concerned about a negative impact on their time/effort. Indeed, since these individuals are apt to have a vested interest in the discussion, they may well have the most to contribute.

What To Do Before The Session

Identify anyone who may be impacted by new initiatives or changes and discuss possible implementation approaches, resources, etc. with them. Aim to satisfy concerns they may have about how implementation may complicate their current job.

If proposed innovations will take more time and effort to implement, develop a plan in advance to resource its implementation. If you already have identified an implementation resource, make that information clear so others won't be worried they will get the job.

To circumvent misunderstandings related to the time/effort filter, circulate your resource plan in advance or be prepared to introduce it at the start of your session.

What To Do During The Session

If you have a specific plan for implementation and how to handle the extra workload, introduce it.

As ideas are generated or implementation and planning/investigation requirements are identified, identify how these will get done. Where possible, identify resources. This approach will reassure participants who may not be sure whether or not they will get the extra work.

During discussions, try to separate the idea generation from the implementation. If possible, save implementation discussions until the end—except when you need to reassure participants that you have it covered.

Sample Situation

You can see that participants are holding back ideas related to what can be done to improve a particular process.

Action

If everyone seems hesitant to address the issue/"keep it real," introduce your plan and identify the person who will do the work. Say something like, "it seems some of you are concerned about workload. Well, I've planned for that and here is how we will get this done. . ."

If you can identify an individual who might be holding back their contribution, ask the person for input—and make it clear they won't get the work. For example, say, "Jane, while you won't have to get involved with investigating the idea, what are the things you would do to validate it?"

Group Think

This filter affects idea generation by encouraging everyone to agree—without really talking or thinking about the topic at hand. Group think kicks in when it seems easier or better to move on with an issue. Those affected may simply want to minimize their risk of being the only one with a contrarian viewpoint. It can also result from issues discussed in the next section, Managing The Personalities. When certain personalities are at work, group think occurs because participants don't want to put forth ideas that might be challenged.

The group think filter undermines idea generation because it encourages participants to abdicate their responsibilities or opinions to the group. They do this to avoid presenting contrary views or because they figure others are better positioned to know the right path to take.

Group think can also be about letting someone else take the risk with new ideas. Here, it makes it easy for individuals to simply "go along" with someone else instead of stretching and coming up with other solutions.

To be clear, group think results from lazy thinking. When one person comes up with an idea that might work, others stop thinking about the problem.

How To Mitigate This Filter

Whenever everyone is thinking the same thing, or if one or two speak out and nobody else bothers to contribute, call on other individuals specifically and challenge them to disagree, even if it's just to test the idea or theory.

Don't let participants off the hook. You should expect them to contribute individually, not just agree with each other.

Even though the ultimate goal is to reach full agreement, use the group process to test the ideas being generated. You don't want to find out, after the fact, that participants had reservations but weren't willing to step up and disagree, even if they foresaw problems.

What To Do Before The Session

Since this filter doesn't merely affect individual participation, there might not be much you can do before the session starts.

One option is to meet individually with those you think will make the most valuable contributions. You may even be able to identify contrarian viewpoints. Ask these individuals to contribute by playing the devil's advocate when others seem too willing to agree.

What To Do During The Session

Step in whenever you see the group think filter set in, including times where participants reach consensus before the topic is fully addressed (they seem too keen to "move on"), or individuals remain silent when you know or believe they have ideas and experiences to contribute.

As a catalyst to developing an alternate view, ask specific questions and challenge current ideas. Avoid open-ended questions that are directed to the group. Instead, address specific questions to specific individuals.

Sample Situation

You ask, "John, what else can you add to the discussion?"

"Nothing else to say," John says.

Let's say you continue asking the others and get similar responses, with almost everyone else agreeing—and not contributing—anything new to the discussion.

Action

While a group consensus may be reached at the end of a session or after everyone else has spoken to a particular issue, you have a problem if this response is what you get early on in the process.

If you exhaust your effort to get additional input, but know individuals are holding back, tell everyone what's happened. Be up front about how the group think filter holds them back from identifying ideas that will positively impact their workplace/process.

Then change the group dynamics by breaking members into two or more teams. Challenge each team to come up with an alternate idea—or one that counters the group think solution. Encourage them to be the devil's advocate. To ease the process, give them a specific situation or scenario to use as a concrete base for their thinking. For instance, you could list the idea that you feel is the result of group think and challenge the separate teams to come up with reasons why it doesn't work and ways to change or improve it.

Have the groups work independently and tell them they are competing with the other groups. Give them a minimum number of ideas they have to come up with before you move on, such as 3 reasons it doesn't work and 3 ways to improve or change it.

Deferral

The deferral filter's power comes from the fact that people don't want to rock the boat or take the effort necessary to argue or advocate for ideas or change. It's easier to agree with others and move on, particularly if the one advocating change (or the status quo) is the boss or someone identified as being the expert.

Deferral occurs when everyone agrees with or defers to the boss or the presumed subject matter expert and is resigned to keeping the status quo or accepting a solution or idea they don't believe in.

This is particularly a problem when dominant participants are the first to talk, especially when they present an idea or position that others are reluctant to challenge.

Many people are hesitant to challenge the boss or someone who is seen as the subject matter expert.

How To Mitigate This Filter

While the boss or expert may be right, the process of idea generation only works when the process is able to fully explore all ideas. There may be a new angle or even part of the idea that will work, literally an idea from the corners.

Instead of letting the group hear from the expert and then moving on to other topics, get the participants to bring ideas forward first. Use these ideas to foster discussion and to explore every idea. Make sure the expert doesn't shut down discussion with authoritative statements.

This approach tells participants that their input is valued. It also ensures that you explore every possible corner before moving on.

Don't let the deferral filter allow you to dismiss potential ideas and solutions before they are explored. The group may well decide an idea isn't the best approach. That realization is much more powerful when the group gets the opportunity to discover it themselves.

What To Do Before The Session

If you know the group includes dominant participants to whom the others will be tempted to defer, speak with these authorities/subject experts in advance. Tell them why you want them to wait until others have spoken. Explain how this approach reduces the impact of deferral by allowing other participants to contribute ideas.

Also ask them to be, and appear to be, fully open to new ideas and challenges to their positions. Remind them that even if they feel they are right, it is still better for everyone else to arrive at the same conclusion through discussion and debate.

If the experts are easily identified, make sure all participants know that the process is meant to solicit different viewpoints and experiences as these are important to shaping positive results. Get the boss or subject matter experts to address the group and clearly state that they are open to new ideas and will help develop and explore those ideas.

What To Do During The Session

If you see deferral happening, step in immediately and challenge those who are deferring to think of ideas that could work. Challenge them to identify roadblocks and ways to overcome them. Urge them to explore even tangential ideas that would work.

Instead of asking questions to the group as a whole, directly ask individuals for their thoughts. Target participants you know would have an opinion or a different experience and challenge them to bring it forward into the discussion.

If the subject matter expert or boss is not cooperating in exploring ideas and is simply saying the ideas presented "won't work" or is insisting their idea is best, you may need to call a break. Take them aside to remind them that they need to be open and foster discussion. If they won't cooperate or you feel their presence itself hinders discussion, you may need to ask them to step out for this part of the exploration process. Invite them back for a final wrap-up of that specific discussion.

Sample Situation

Let's say a participant comes up with an idea or solution and the subject matter expert says, "that won't work, I know because I tried it."

This statement cuts off discussion as other participants defer to the subject matter expert.

Action

First, challenge the subject matter expert to agree that perhaps there may be different approaches that could make it work and they are worth exploring. Even if they are hesitant to concede this point, stay the course and take the discussion to the next step.

Speak to the other participants directly and prompt them to discuss the idea and see what could be done to make it work. Engage the subject matter expert for details on their perspective and work through different situations, scenarios or approaches. Then evaluate whether a different outcome may be reached.

If the subject matter expert is still reluctant or putting up roadblocks, split the team into two groups. Ask the group that includes the expert to identify all the challenges and the reasons the idea will fail.

Ask the second group to come up with specific items they would do differently to make the idea/new process succeed.

Bring the two groups together and cross reference the two lists, then debate both sides until you get ideas that will work or everyone agrees there is no viable solution.

If a subject expert is not cooperating and you feel it is necessary for the process to continue, ask that person to sit out the discussion.

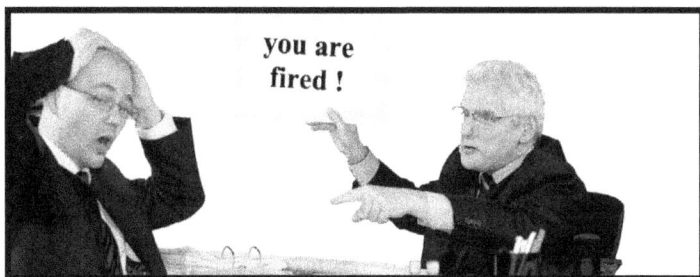

you are
fired !

Risk Aversion

How much risk you are willing to take on defines how far you can stretch within your circle and box. The risk aversion filter can have personal and business implications. When you and your team don't look at ideas and solutions that may present risk, you limit your ability to improve results.

Risk aversion is a powerful motivator and an influential filter.

A personal risk, such as job security, creates the kind of filter that promotes sabotage and decreases authentic participation.

Participants identify as "risky" ideas that may fail, foster ridicule, cause harm related to disagreeing with the boss or impair their work environment through implementation.

How To Mitigate This Filter

If the risks perceived are not realistic, reassure participants of your intent in making sure they won't happen. You may not convince everyone, so keep an eye individual participation and mitigate as needed.

When there are real risks (to participants' jobs, reputations, etc.), be aware of the impact and mitigate the negative fallout by carefully planning your sessions. If these risks are not managed, participants could sabotage your efforts to generate ideas. (This might not even be intentional. Fear is a powerful motivator.)

What To Do Before The Session

If you think legitimate risks may exist, or that participants may perceive them, speak confidentially with the participants to pinpoint the issues.

This gives you more information about the risks participants have identified. Now use that data to design the session to reduce the filtering that comes from risk aversion.

Where possible, address identified risks in advance or with specific individuals. This lets you manage real risks and eliminates aversion to perceived but non-existent risks.

If you can't address the risk in advance, design the sessions to mitigate the risk aversion. This may include anonymous input, deciding not to have the boss present or telling participants they can only bring forward solutions or ideas that have everyone's agreement. These strategies give individuals some protection from risks associated with their honest participation.

If the risk is to a specific individual, such as making their position redundant, carefully manage their participation and input to make sure the individual doesn't sabotage the session and process. If sabotage occurs, you may need to exclude that individual from the sessions or develop and communicate an acceptable alternative for them. (If their position is negatively impacted but there is room for a linear move, let them know that's part of the plan.)

What To Do During The Session

If you were able to mitigate the risk or at least the perception of risk by individual participants, you should be able to conduct the session normally.

If not, you could use an anonymous method for the initial idea generation and then use the group to work through the ideas provided With this option, you do not require anyone to take credit (or responsibility) for the idea or solution. Here, all must agree to maintain session confidentiality—even after solutions are put into place.

You could also meet separately with each participant to get their input and thoughts, then summarize them for the group session. This approach maintains confidentiality of the initial ideas and issues raised and it may make your participants more comfortable about working through the process and arriving at an agreement. They will get to see the compiled information, but they won't be identified with contributing specific ideas, solutions or points of discussion.

Sample Situation

You know the jobs of certain participants may be negatively impacted by your session.

Action

To mitigate how this information may lead to the implementation of the risk aversion filter, you need to have a plan in place for the affected employee or employees. Communicate that plan to the individuals who may be impacted.

An advance discussion (pre-session) will be required to avoid the possibility of a negative reaction and potential sabotage by affected participants who might block ideas or misrepresent issues.

Sample Situation

Ideas are not being brought forward because they may conflict with or deviate from what is considered to be the company's or boss's agenda.

Action

If the boss is in the session, find a reason for him or her to leave so participants won't be intimidated by that individual's presence.

If the potentially problematic issue involves a general topic (e.g., accounting procedures, equipment maintenance, past practices), frame the discussion so that participants realize the session and its topic were sanctioned by the organization precisely because it needs to be addressed or new ideas are sought to challenge the current wisdom and direction. In other words, if participants can find something better, the company will benefit. Indeed, even knowing that the current way is best allows the company to proceed with confidence.

Quick Summary

Key Points	➡ Your staff aren't the only ones with filters—be careful to get rid of your own filters, too.
	➡ People don't usually recognize that they have filters.
Executive Tips	➡ Filters can't be dropped just because you tell your team they should. It takes effort and strategy.
	➡ Don't be shy to call someone out for their filter and get them to re-examine their thinking.
Traps to Avoid	➡ Don't allow someone's filters to influence discussion.

Your Plan

Based on what you've read, what will you do to develop creative ideas and solutions to improve results?

What are you going to do?	When

Notes

_____

_____

_____

_____

_____

_____

_____

_____

_____

_____

_____

_____

Managing the Personalities

Effectively drawing out ideas while
preventing their suppression is
necessary for creativity.

*"Thinking is the hardest work there is,
which is probably the reason so few engage
in it." ~ Henry Ford*

In addition to the self-imposed filters that limit our ability to stretch into the corners, the group dynamic involved with developing new ideas is also a factor in how far we stretch into the corners of our respective boxes.

This comes down to personality as well as background. While each team member can contribute to ideas, the presence of others sometimes limits our willingness to put ourselves out there and identify stretch ideas.

The personality types that serve as negative filters to the group process include:

➡ Dominator
➡ The Authority
➡ Expert
➡ Saboteur
➡ Wallflower

The facilitator needs to take the dynamics of these personality types into account and make sure they don't restrict or limit creativity of the group as a whole.

You can do this by considering the people who will be in your sessions and then figuring out who may have which personality type, or could be perceived as having a particular type. In some cases, you may need to discuss the issue with individuals in advance of the session. You could, for example, ask them to adjust their behaviour or approach.

You are also likely to have to deal with these issues during your facilitated session. Be perceptive about how they act as filters and use the techniques identified to minimize their impact.

On rare occasions, you may find it better to keep someone from participating if you know they will have a negative impact. If they are an important part of the team, you will have to meet with them, post-session, to address the solutions and issues generated at the session. This may be the only way to gain their input and buy-in.

The following section takes a closer look at the key personalities that can negatively impact how well your team stretches into the corners during group sessions.

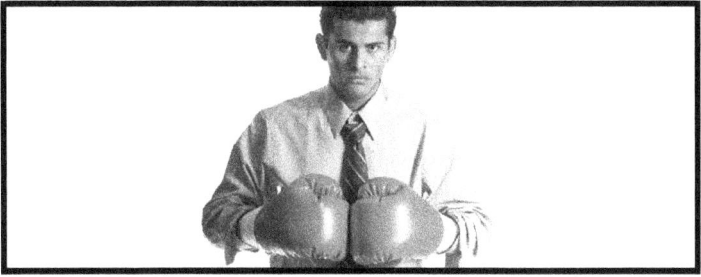

Dominator

This personality type intimidates others and prevents them from contributing. The dominator's persuasiveness is usually related to their perceived expertise or their forceful and opinionated personality.

When a dominant or aggressive member with strong opinions is at work in a group, many participants will filter their ideas if they think they'll have to argue or disagree with this person.

Others will simply become weary of the process and stop contributing. This decreases the session's value by inhibiting a more open and honest discussion.

How To Mitigate This Filter

The facilitator should try to identify members of the group who possess a dominant personality — and take action. Where possible, talk to the individual before the session and attempt to prevent dominator-type behaviour. The dominator may not be aware of his or her behaviour or its impact on others. Bringing it to their attention may be the easiest solution.

If the individual doesn't cooperate, it may be necessary to hold the session without them present.

Identifying a dominator is usually quite easy. These individuals are often the first to speak on a topic and their enthusiasm (pro or con) for a position may decrease input from others. At other times, they may attack ideas presented by other participants, again discouraging input from others.

What To Do Before The Session

Identify who may be a dominator and speak with them before the session. Explain how their approach may impact others and ask them to hold back their opinions or encourage others.

Tell them you know this trait can work as a filter for others in the group. Let them know you will step in and ask them to hold their comments if you see an issue, but they should not take this personally as it's not the only personality trait filter you will be managing. Sometimes a gentle reminder is all that is needed.

If you feel the individual's track record or attitude won't enable you to control the session and suppress the dominator's impact, hold the session without them.

What To Do During The Session

If you see a dominant personality taking control or inhibiting others from contributing during a session, call a break when practical. Use that time to discuss the issue with the dominating individual. If you discussed this earlier, remind them you foresaw their might be a problem. If this is the first time you've addressed the issue personally, make them aware of how this trait impacts others and works against generating ideas. Ask them to hold back their comments and critiques.

If the individual continues to dominate, call on other individuals and specifically ask for their input. Where possible, use closed questions to solicit specifics rather than an open-ended question they can avoid in deference to the dominator. (Ask: "How would you shorten the time required between these two activities", not "What would you do to shorten the total time?")

It may be necessary to ask the dominant personality to leave the session if they don't cooperate. Do this discretely and give them an "out" by telling others the individual had to leave to attend other business.

Sample Situation

During the session, Jack always interrupts others to insert his opinion and does not let the others finish their thoughts.

Action

Interrupt Jack when he does this and ask him to wait until others have spoken.

If you can, take Jack aside during a break and tell him that while his input is valuable, the intent of the meeting is to seek alternatives. Encourage Jack to contribute in a positive way. Acknowledge his interest in participating and ask him to comment on how the ideas being presented might work, versus won't work.

If all else fails, discretely ask Jack to leave the session.

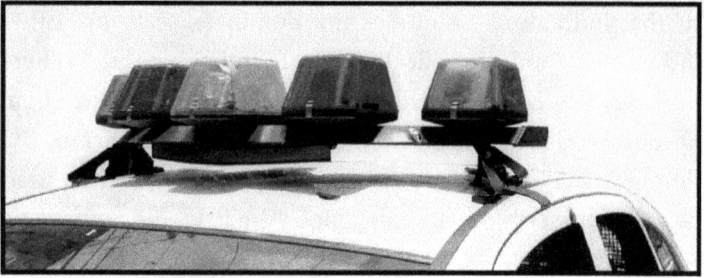

The Authority

Someone with an authority personality trait can also play a filtering role by inhibiting others from contributing ideas.

An authority is usually the boss or a senior person with whom others are hesitant to disagree or present contrary views. Some participants defer to the authority by waiting for that individual's opinion before making a contribution of their own. (They test the water before jumping in.)

This differs from the dominant personality by virtue of organizational position. Although their impact may be similar, a dominator may not have a position power.

When this filter's at work, creative ideas and solutions that could have a negative impact on the authority or their position are in particular danger of suppression. Where ideas expressed through the group process differ from ideas the authority expresses, participants may even change their positions or opinions if they believe the authority's favour is at risk.

How To Mitigate This Filter

If possible, it's usually preferable to not include the authority in the group session. This will reduce—or eliminate—the potentially negative impact.

That's because this filter comes into play with presence versus behaviour. While the person in authority may be able to put aside self-interest when participating in a group session, it is foolish to assume that others in the group will forget that person's authoritative role.

Even if the authority figure participates as an observer and doesn't contribute, that person's presence can make others in the room hesitant to speak up.

This can happen no matter how amiable or open the authority figure appears to be.

What To Do Before The Session

Again, may be best to not have authority figures at a group session that's meant to generate innovative ideas. These people can receive and comment on the results or be involved in a follow-up session.

If they must be involved from the outset, ask the authority to encourage alternate views and to acknowledge the validity of these views. As this situation is not ideal, be mindful of how their presence may impact results.

What To Do During the Session

If authority figures must be involved in the session, prepare them as noted above. Encourage them to support the generation of new ideas.

For this situation to work, authority figures must actively support the honest sharing of information. A passive or silent approach might not reduce the impact of their presence.

Look for opportunities to facilitate this support. Early in the session, when you draw out an idea or opinion that may be seen as contrary to the authority's position, ask the authority to comment. If you have prepared them well and they cooperate, a positive response from them will help mitigate any negative influence based on their presence and participation.

If a participant clearly changes his position to agree with the authority, ask that participant about the change. Encourage him to be honest about the factors involved. (This can help authority figures understand how their presence can keep people from reaching outside of their circles and into the corners of the box.)

Sample Situation

John presents an idea that is directly contrary to the direction the department currently takes.

Action

Turn to Ellen, the department head and say, "Ellen, that's very different from your current direction. What do you think of John's idea?"

Ellen should say something like, "Yes, it is different, but that's why I want John's opinion. As long as change is for the better, I am open to seeing where this might take us."

Saboteur

The saboteur personality trait serves as a negative filter to the group process when a participant actively works to counter any progress made at the session. Saboteurs often try to suppress new and creative ideas to maintain the status quo.

In addition to favouring the status quo, the saboteur may have an agenda to guide the results in a particular direction.

Saboteurs sometimes feel they are at risk with change. They may want to hold onto a position they think makes them "look good" to an authority. Others may want to avoid having to expend effort to implement a new idea.

This causes them to directly or indirectly sabotage any process linked to change.

Instead of making a positive contribution, saboteurs always take a negative position and find reasons to argue why something can't work.

Some saboteurs behave this way because change—and the potential for change—might impact them directly or be contrary to their agenda. Other saboteurs may simply act this way because it's their personality. They like being contrarians.

How To Mitigate This Filter

This type of person will seriously dampen others' contributions and threaten your ability to find solutions and ideas that push into the corners of your organizational box.

Identifying the saboteurs before a session is the best way to deal with them effectively. Once you know who they are, you must decide if they need to be kept out of the session. If that's not possible, you will need a plan to monitor and counter their impact.

What To Do Before The Session

When possible, don't invite saboteurs to the session.

If they must attend the session, meet with them beforehand to discuss their approach and how it is likely to impact results. Let them know you will ask them to stop behaviour that negatively impacts the session.

What To Do During The Session

If they participate, take a firm position with them from the outset of the session. Cut them off when they start to go in a negative or counter-productive direction.

If you see that they are taking positions that align with an agenda, use your facilitation role to counter those positions or call them out, in a polite way, during the session. Bring facts, observations and experiences from others into the discussion.

Sample Situation

Alex continually puts forward a particular idea or solution. She then fights for it, but offers dubious support. Instead of working with the group on new ideas she keeps arguing for a position others don't like and can't—or won't—support.

Action

You can say "Alex, I think you've done a great job of making us aware of your position on that topic. However, we've moved on and have agreed to put a different idea forward. I know you can contribute your experience to making the consensus idea work. Since you have identified the hurdles you feel exist, what can we do to overcome them?"

If Alex continues to sabotage the process, you should quietly speak with him at the next break and give him a choice. He can be silent, contribute to the solution or leave. You may have to apply pressure to get the result you want. This may involve enlisting his boss's support or indicating you have no choice but to challenge his motives.

Wallflowers

Wallflowers don't fully participate in the session. They often hold back ideas and don't express their thoughts on subjects directly related to their work.

This personality trait filter sweeps valuable thoughts and ideas under the table. What's not spoken is also not acknowledged.

Wallflower behaviour is complicated in that it can be influenced by the existence of other personality trait filters in the group, including those linked to authority and dominator personalities. Other times, the wallflower individual simply prefers to be in the background, lacks confidence or doesn't think he or she is qualified to contribute.

People with this trait may also be more intimidated by the more gregarious personalities of other group participants. Again, this makes them more hesitant to contribute.

How To Mitigate This Filter

The most productive way to reduce the impact of the wallflower filter is to decrease the influence of the other personality trait filters.

Rather than forcing the wallflower to open up, find ways for them to contribute that do not make them uncomfortable.

What To Do Before The Session

If you know them to be quiet individuals, speak with them in advance and encourage their participation. Where appropriate, address their concerns about other participants or try to find out why they don't feel qualified to speak on the topic.

Sometimes wallflowers are more willing to express themselves in a one-on-one discussion before a session. If that's the case, draw out their ideas and thoughts and then share these ideas in the session. You don't have to identify where the ideas came from and the individual won't have to speak up.

What To Do during The Session

Manage the session so that when these individuals contribute, there is no negative response. Rather than wait for them to volunteer ideas, try calling upon them specifically.

Don't, however, make them uncomfortable or press them to contribute if they clearly don't want to.

Sometimes people who don't actively contribute to a session will be able to provide interesting perspectives on the proceedings by virtue of how closely they listen to what others have to say. Try to seek out these individuals during session breaks, or after the session is complete. They may offer valuable insights that can help your process.

Sample Situation

During a session, you realize that one participant never contributes to the discussion. When you call on them, they resist or say they have nothing to add.

Action

Since this is unexpected and you were not able to address the matter before the session started, speak with the individual at the next break. Try to find out why they are not contributing.

If you can, mitigate the filter for this individual. Encourage their participation, acknowledge how they may be impacted by other personalities in the room and let them know you will work to decrease the impact of issues related to those other personality filters. (If possible, speak privately with a dominator or authority, or address the issues those more assertive personalities can cause when the session reconvenes.)

If you can't mitigate the filter, or it is simply a personality or confidence issue, tell them you still want their candid input. If they do share it with you, tell them you would be happy to express those thoughts with the group without revealing where the information came from.

Expert

An individual with the expert personality trait may not be open to new ideas. This will suppress discussion and your team's ability to think into the corners. Others may see the expert's opinions as the only ideas worth listening to. They will give up looking for alternatives—creating filter problems closely related to those caused by the authority filter.

The expert can be someone with recognized expertise or an individual who is forceful enough to make people think they are an expert.

If the group includes cross-functional participants, those without the expertise of these subject matter individuals will be hesitant to speak up and contribute.

In addition, the expert may unintentionally dominate because they're able to speak with confidence and details.

How To Mitigate This Filter

Experts can feel challenged when alternate views and ideas are brought forward. A high regard for their knowledge and expertise may also prompt others to steer clear of ideas that might challenge the expert. Use this to your advantage during sessions.

What To Do Before The Session

Ask the expert to reassure other participants that while they may be an expert, they welcome—and can learn from—outside views.

If this is unlikely to work because of the individual's personality, speak with them in advance and acknowledge their expertise. Ask them to apply that expertise to explore how alternate ideas can be successful instead of how they might fail.

It sometimes may seem counter intuitive, but you should exclude the expert from the discussions if you can't count on them to cooperate with the process. Their expertise will be a hindrance rather than a benefit. You can always solicit their input in a more controlled way after the session.

What To Do During The Session

If the expert dominates discussion and others stop adding ideas and their own thoughts, ask the expert to wait until everyone else has finished before speaking.

If they won't cooperate, ask them to leave the session. If that doesn't work, or is not possible, tactfully but forcefully challenge them in the session. Ask the expert to justify his or her position, prove how a new idea won't work, etc. This is a risky approach, but you may need to take it.

Sample Situation

After some discussion, Steve says, "okay, let's stop right now. This won't work, you are all wrong. I know better than anyone here, so we need to move on."

Action

Instead of arguing, tell Steve, "we know you are the expert. That's why you're here, to lend that expertise to finding new solutions. If we implemented that idea anyway, what you would you do, as the expert, to make sure you succeeded? Remember, we're counting on your expertise to succeed. With that in mind, tell us what you would you do to make it work?"

If Steve refuses to make a positive contribution and you need more discussion about the idea, ask him to list the 5 main barriers to success. Then break up the team into smaller groups to address those barriers. Exclude Steve from this part of the process. Do take Steve aside and tell him that he needs to provide a constructive contribution to the results or stay silent until the session concludes. Be positive. Remind him that this is a *process*, not a race with a specific finish line. Let him know you will explore his issues with him independently after the session.

Quick Summary

Key Points

➡ The personalities of participants can keep others from stretching into the corners.

➡ Personalities can be dealt with if you recognize the behaviour.

➡ Often, people don't realize the impact they have on others. Once they understand, they are likely to adjust how they act.

Executive Tips

➡ If a team member's behaviour is detrimental to the team, don't let them participate in the main meeting.

➡ You may be one of the personalities that negatively impacts others, particularly if you are the boss. If so, consider not participating.

Traps to Avoid

➡ Don't excuse a personality's impact because they are seen to be "indispensable" to the process.

Your Plan

Based on what you've read, what will you do to develop creative ideas and solutions to improve results?

What are you going to do?	When

Notes

Tools For Stretching Into The Corners

Successfully developing and fostering ideas from your team improves your success.

> *"It's not the tools that you have faith in —*
> *tools are just tools. They work, or they don't*
> *work. It's people you have faith in or not." ~*
> *Steve Jobs*

The way you set up your creative problem-solving exercise can have a direct impact on whether you are able to generate the kind of solutions and ideas that are practical and can be implemented.

This focus on the process *environment* will help you get much more value from the principles of *Thinking Into The Corners*.™ It does this by helping you get the most from a range of idea-generating tools and techniques with which you are already familiar.

The value of using tried and true techniques is that you know they work. But learning more about how they work in different situations—and for different types of problem solving—dramatically improves your ability to apply the ones that work best for your specific issues and group dynamics.

Facilitated Sessions

Teamwork and collaboration solicit better ideas than efforts that focus solely on individuals trying to work out solutions on their own.

But calling a meeting to address the problem and putting a bunch of people together and hoping for the best won't work. Progress—and success—require a planned, structured approach that has·a purpose, uses the right techniques and ends with a specific action plan.

While you should, of course, use a variety of tools to generate ideas (these are discussed below), sessions like this begin with structure. Your framework should create a formal session that is facilitated to keep it on-time and on-track. A capable facilitator should also remove or mitigate as many negative filters as possible. This creates an environment that favours the generation of new ideas.

While you can facilitate your team's session, it is better to engage someone who's not invested in the issue. Bringing in a facilitator from a different department (such as human resources) or from an outside organization, allows you to fully contribute to the session. Instead of managing the process, you can be part of it.

Facilitation includes establishing the goals and objectives, planning idea-generating activities using proven tools and selecting the participants. Some advance preparation to understand the participants will help the facilitator identify underlying group dynamics and potential trouble spots. This is important to setting and then managing the ground rules of the session.

Applying It To The Corners

When conducting group sessions using *Thinking Into The Corners™*, facilitation is a key element in getting participants to fully participate so the end result pushes past the group's circle limits and into the corners.

The facilitator must be aware of how box and circle limits impact discussion and progress. They should focus discussion with that in mind. While the circle limits are fairly traditional and should be considered in any kind of group session, the principles of thinking into the corners will be new.

Helping the group define the box limits—and then introducing the notion of box limit *expansion*—needs to be an expressed focus of the session. The facilitator must make this innovative into-the-corners strategy a priority, not assume it will happen naturally.

Cross-Functional Groups

If managed properly, a cross-functional group will solve problems and develop ideas much better than a group consisting of the same types of functions or expertise. This approach helps to reduce some of the filters that come from being too close to the topic or issue. Staff from different functional areas may see issues and solutions that aren't apparent to the people who've been doing the job for many years.

At the same time, there is a risk that some of the ideas generated could miss the mark because their proponents lack some of the knowledge or insight of those working in that area. This is a trade-off that's well worth it, but you do need to manage the process properly and prepare the group before you start. You do not want the functional experts, for example, to misunderstand the process or to dismiss or ridicule ideas coming from other staff members.

Combining this approach with some of the other tools will minimize the filtering and enable new ideas to be explored no matter how far off they seem to their colleagues. Sometimes ideas that won't work as first introduced can lead to the development of concepts that can be adjusted and applied with great success. As always, it's important to develop an open mind within the group and minimize the filters.

Applying It To The Corners

One of the biggest potential problems with cross-functional groups is how they might naturally strengthen the filters that could negatively impact results. Facilitators must be mindful of this issue.

Brainstorming

Once you have your facilitator and have chosen your cross-functional group (paying special attention to filters and personality traits), brainstorming is often the best way to start developing ideas. It is a tried-and-true approach that is easily applied to thinking into the corners.

Remember to keep the brainstorming within the box limits and to consider how individuals and the group are affected by circle limits and personalities. You want to eliminate some filters—and manage the others.

Brainstorming can be used for at least two parts of the process. First, use brainstorming techniques to explore and expand the box limits as much as possible. This approach might be all that's needed to generate workable solutions.

After you expand the box limits, use brainstorming to go after the ideas or solutions it generated. Get participants to seek solutions in the corners instead of outside the box. The idea with brainstorming is to get ideas on the table without discussing them first (i.e. green lighting).

Since your focus is on idea generation, this strategy increases the number of ideas presented and makes it less likely that ideas will be suppressed by discussion, argument or dissention. Once you're done generating ideas, vigorously discuss those ideas but keep the focus on ideas that can work within the box limits. As dynamic discussion may identify new ways to expand the box limits, always leave open the option to inflate those limits. Remember: the limits are real but you're reaching into corners and that process can shift the boundaries.

The brainstorming process can be very difficult for a group to do well, particularly if individual members are used to giving their opinions and approach the process with strong technical expertise or entrenched attitudes about the issues on the table. (It's hard to "unknow" what you are sure to be true.)

Counter these issues by setting clear ground rules and then be diligent in applying them. Whenever anyone starts to assess somebody else's idea, simply ask them to reserve their comments for the follow-up process. Let participants know you want the process to run its course and are not trying to silence dissention. They may not know that brainstorming works best when participants don't jump ahead of the process. Pay close attention to the circle limits, including filters and personalities. Eliminate or manage these issues to defeat their limiting influence.

Brainstorming is, of course, a collection of idea-generating techniques.

What follows is a discussion of several methods you can use to generate ideas in a brainstorming session. If you are leading a brainstorming session to deal with expanding the box limits, remember to conduct the process, be it round table, break-out groups or blind ideas, separately for each side of the box.

Round Table

The round table approach to brainstorming works particularly well with smaller groups. With larger groups, getting input from everyone can take too much time and those who speak last may find their ideas have already been covered.

When establishing the box limits, focus on each side of the box in separate rounds of the brainstorming. Larger groups can be split into sub-groups that focus on specific box limits. The entire group can then help with the review.

Just be sure to give participants enough time to prepare for what you're going to ask. Without preparation, the first participant you call on will be disadvantaged since they didn't have any time to think about it.

You will also need to acknowledge that the last ones to talk may not have anything new to contribute.

One value of the round table approach is that it forces everyone involved to be prepared and to contribute at least one solution when it's their turn to talk. This can be particularly helpful to those who may otherwise hesitate to contribute. However, don't force shy or reserved participants to contribute in this very public way, particularly if they may not be in a position to suggest solutions. (For particular strategies with these individuals, refer back to the wallflower section discussed in Managing the Personalities.)

Break-Out Groups

Break-out groups are a great way to develop ideas when you're working with a large group. They also give participants who are less likely to contribute on their own, a better opportunity to support the process.

When using break-out groups separate the entire group into smaller groups of participants and give them time to collectively come up with their ideas and suggestions.

Don't let the groups form without input from you and, if necessary, an external facilitator. Strategically select participants for each group based on the knowledge, background and personality of each person. This will yield the best results.

While the groups are working, the facilitator should circulate and ensure they are making progress and that everyone is contributing. Watch for individuals who dominate the discussion and for other personalities or filters that might inhibit the discussion.

Once they are finished, have each group select a representative to share their ideas with the larger group.

Again, you can have the break-out groups each focus on all sides of the box, or on a specific box limit. When they present their ideas, facilitate more discussion from other groups.

Blind Ideas

You can use this technique if you want the ideas to be anonymous or have reason to believe that a number of participants will hesitate to speak in front of the group.

Give the participants time to think and to write down their ideas on pieces of paper that they can put inside a basket or box. Then pick the papers from the box and read them out. Do not identify the individual unless he or she wants to talk about the idea. Have someone else write the ideas on a pad board. If ideas are contributed by more than one individual, combine them into one, but keep track of how many people came up with the idea.

Consider This

If you are leading a brainstorming session to deal with expanding the box limits, conduct the process separately for each side of the box.

Applying It To The Corners

Brainstorming techniques are a sound way to develop ideas and solutions. The tool is easily applied to the principles of

Thinking Into The Corners™, but you must develop and run your brainstorming session with the box limits in mind.

If the process generates ideas that are outside the box limits (even after expansion), park those items outside the box for now. You may want to use some time to explore how the box might be expanded to accommodate the new idea. But don't forget that your focus on workable solutions means you are purposefully working inside the box. If an idea doesn't fit into those parameters, move on.

Exploration

The exploration part of an idea-generating session is essentially the brainstorming (or "what if?") portion of the process. It helps the group fully explore ideas and solutions and assess and address any problems. When appropriate, exploration may lead us abandon a proposed solution before too much time is spent on an idea you cannot put into action. Exploration begins after you have arrived at one or more solutions that appear viable.

Exploration is the opposite of a "green light" session. Here, participants try and identify as many valid "red lights'"' as possible. They look for problems, issues, roadblocks and limitations that will affect the viability of the solution.

It is important to discuss how red lights can be solved. In the end, you want to have as few "red lights" as possible.

Some of the "red lights" may be easily solved through discussion. Others may have to be explored outside of the discussion. But once you've identified the problem, you should also be on track to overcome them—especially if the solution is inside the box limits.

Applying It To The Corners

Since this tool helps you identify roadblocks (including even box limits) it is more of an input than an output to your overall process.

However, once you start looking for solutions, you need to apply the principles of *Thinking Into The Corners*™.

Ask 5 Sequential Questions

With this exploration-related technique, the facilitator asks questions and probes deep enough to challenge assumptions to get at the real answer to the issue. This approach goes beyond the superficial.

Do this separately for each side of the box when you are expanding the limits. Once you've established the box limits, ask questions directly related to the issue or problem you are trying to solve.

When you ask yourself or your team these questions, you are probing for answers and are not assuming the response.

The key is to ask questions related to the answer to the previous question. When you get the first answer, ask another question about that answer. This variation of the fishbone technique often used in problem solving can also be used in your process to document the key information you need from each of the questions.

Go several levels deep in your questioning. If you are writing it as you go, be sure to start on a large whiteboard or paper tacked to the wall, enabling you to expand it with more paper if necessary.

Here is an example of how asking sequential questions builds on previous answers to develop a more complete response:

1. What is important to the occupant?

2. For each of the items that are important, why are they important?

3. For each reason they are important, what is the risk of failure? What is the benefit of succeeding?

4. For each of the risks items, how can they be minimized or eliminated?

5. For each of the risk items, what do we do to minimize risk that benefits the occupant?

As the reasons a problem exists are not necessarily apparent, questions like this make it easier for you to get at what's really happening. Unless you dig deeper, you won't be able to implement a solution that will work.

Another application of the sequential question approach can also help you pinpoint the root cause of an issue.

Step	Question	Answer
1	Why wasn't the work order completed on-time?	The technician had to go back a second time to finish the job.
2	Why did he have to go back?	The tech didn't have the tools he needed.
3	Why didn't he have the tools?	The work order didn't have the information the tech needed to select the right tools.

Step	Question	Answer	
4	Why didn't it have the information?	**A**	The help desk rep doesn't have the background needed to ask the right questions of the customer and write down the information.
		B	The technician didn't ask for more information or call the occupant.
A5	Why don't they have the background?	They were hired as administrative positions and then their role changed.	
A6	Why weren't they trained?	Nobody thought about training them since they were already part of the team.	
A7	How can we fix it?	Provide training.	
B5	Why didn't the technician get more information before going on site?	Most of the time they have the tools they need. Getting information on a work order is too hard.	
B6	Why is it too hard to get information?	They are on the road and it's hard to get answers.	
B7	Why is it hard to get answers?	The help desk staff always have to call them back and they can't answer the phone when they are driving, causing a lot of	

Step	Question	Answer
		telephone tag.
B8	How can we fix it?	Add texting or email plans to the phones so the help desk can simply send them the information.

Once you finish this exercise, you will have the information you need to develop a solution, whether it's details and examples, or a better overall understanding about the issues and requirements.

Applying It To The Corners

Again, this is a universal tool, like brainstorming, so you simply need to apply the new concepts to the process. Monitor the answers and ensure they are within the box limits and be on the lookout for filters that restrict ideas that are in the corners.

Fishbone Diagram

Sometimes, a diagram is the most effective way to illustrate and explore the results of the sequential questioning exercise described above. Diagrams are particularly useful when the questions yield several answers—or several problems that need follow-up.

Tracking these separate issues using other methods can be very cumbersome. Something like the fishbone diagram, however, enables you to follow many different paths of questions and answers using an illustration that is easy to visualize.

You can write out the fishbone diagram on paper on the wall, large post-it notes or a whiteboard. You can even use software to do it electronically.

The bottom line is that a fishbone diagram is a useful way to explore and follow various paths that will eventually take you to the root cause of the problem—and deliver real-world solutions.

Consider This

A fishbone diagram is very easy to use, but be sure to start it on a large enough paper taped to the wall or on a large whiteboard.

The sample below is based on the earlier example of problems with technicians having to visit a work site more than once. Here, the problem is shown in the box at the front of the diagram. Each time you arrive at the end of a particular path, usually with a solution or action item, you can add a circle to keep track. You'll notice that in this case, there are three solutions. In some cases, action is required on all three. Other times, one choice makes the others redundant. Keep an open mind because the best problem-solving action will depend on your specific situation.

To illustrate the technique, we simply identified that there may be other causes for the problem beyond the one we dealt with. In most cases, those other causes should also be explored.

To create your fishbone diagram, draw a line across the middle of a page or whiteboard and write down the problem in a box at the end.

Then ask the first question and draw a line at an angle off the original line and write the short answer on the line. Ask another question, draw another line and write the short answer on that line. Ask more questions and continue to add the lines, with space between them, until your diagram looks like a fishbone.

Now go back to each of the fishbone branches. Draw horizontal lines off the branches and ask another question about the original answer. Write that second answer on the line. Continue the process until you have probed enough to have all the information you need to find a solution.

Your diagram will eventually look similar to the example shown here:

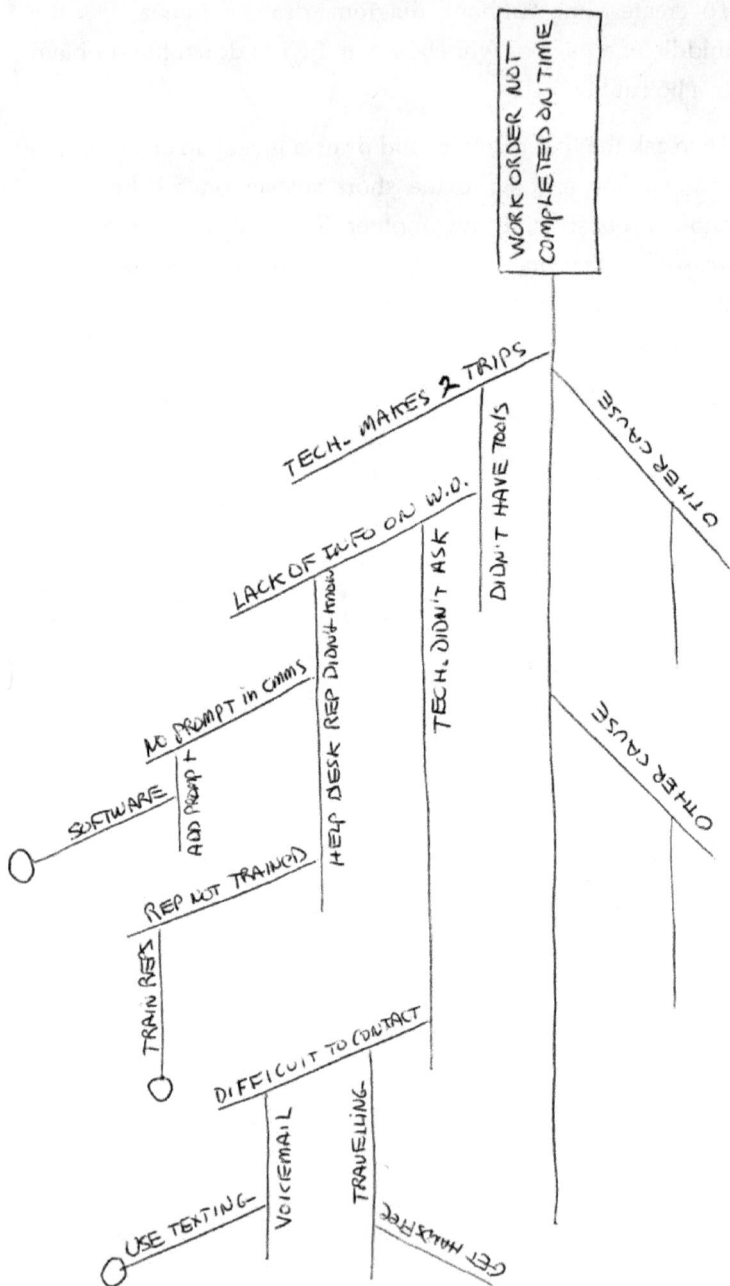

WORK ORDER NOT COMPLETED ON TIME

TECH. MAKES 2 TRIPS

OTHER CAUSE

LACK OF INFO ON W.O.

DIDN'T HAVE TOOLS

NO PROMPT IN CMMS

HELP DESK REP DIDN'T know

TECH. DIDN'T ASK

OTHER CAUSE

SOFTWARE

ADD PROMPT

REP NOT TRAINED

TRAIN REPS

DIFFICULT TO CONTACT

VOICEMAIL

TRAVELLING

USE TEXTING

GET MAX-REC

Applying It To The Corners

With this tool, you are looking for problems, processes, activities, etc. that are causing a problem. The application of *Thinking Into The Corners*™ comes from the solutions you find for those problems. When you start that process, make sure participants stay within the box limits and the filters aren't preventing creative ideas and contribution.

Flowcharts

Whenever you look at processes and interfaces, you need to understand what's happening today and then probe for the problem areas, roadblocks and pressure points that prevent those processes and interfaces from working better. A simple flowchart diagram may be the best way to approach the exploration process. A visual representation of the problem always helps participants improve their understanding of process—and that information alone may reveal where the solution is needed.

The flowchart doesn't have to be complicated. Start with a simple chart that covers the main processes and steps. Where needed, break them down into sub-processes on a different whiteboard or paper. (This is better than creating a large, unmanageable flowchart.)

If you create the flowcharts in a group setting, you may also find that there is some confusion about the process and interfaces. If the process reveals those gaps, aim for group agreement on process and interfaces before proceeding.

Sometimes it makes more sense to develop the flowcharts before the group work begins. If you take this approach, have the group follow the process from start to finish and make sure you all agree on the flow. Again, this will help identify gaps between how processes are being done—and how people *think* they are being done. Agreeing on what must (or should) happen is a great start to improving the processes.

Applying It To The Corners

Like the fishbone diagram, the flowchart is a tool to find out what is happening today and explore the issues. When it starts to lead you to solutions is the time to think about the box limits and filters.

SWOT Analysis

Strength, Weakness, Opportunity, Threat (SWOT) analysis is another common tool for business planning and you can use a modified version to help develop or validate ideas you come up with through other processes. SWOT allows you to explore ideas and solutions to problems.

SWOT analysis can be focused directly on an issue you need to deal with. It can also be used to assess the ideas you have identified as worth of exploration.

The outcome of a SWOT analysis should support the specific problem, issue or strategic plan you are working on. It's the only reason you're doing it, so keep the end goal in mind throughout the process. If you start to look at things in your SWOT analysis that are outside your original goal, park those issues for a future session. While it's always tempting to expand the SWOT session beyond your intended goal, be prepared to manage your time and the involvement of the participants.

Strength

Strengths are related to the solution, problem or issue you are working on. A strength may be directly related to your needs. They can be a direct benefit or advantage of a particular solution or approach. Ideally, a strength will be quantifiable, if not immediately, then with time and study.

If you and your group have a hard time establishing a strength, go through the attributes of the solution or approach you are exploring and try to figure out if it really is a strength. If it's not, move discussion of this solution or approach to another part of the SWOT analysis.

Weakness

Use the same list of attributes from the strengths and look at each one carefully to find weaknesses. These may be related to cost, time, risk or any of the traditional characteristics you would use for decision making.

Once you've identified weaknesses, address them immediately. This may allow you to remove them as a weakness. If it's not possible to overcome a particular weakness right away, put it on a list you can assess later.

Whenever possible, quantify the weakness and identify their importance and impact on the idea's success.

Consider This

Where immediate action on a SWOT item can yield immediate results—take it. If possible, track improvements to make a business case for your leadership skills. Even small changes should be recognized for their incremental value.

Opportunities

Identify the opportunities from the idea or solution you are dealing with in terms of the immediate issue and its spin-off benefits. Where benefits extend beyond the FM department, take credit for having a positive impact on your organization.

As with the weaknesses, quantify opportunities when possible, either during this process or after you've completed the SWOT analysis. This is information you'll use for your business case to demonstrate its value and sell the initiative.

Threats

Threats are essentially risks and problems that could happen if you implement new initiatives, or fail to take action.

Being honest about the threats is important, since these have to be dealt with if you are going to have a successful implementation. You can also develop your response and mitigation to the threats and include them in your business case. Identifying threats and showing your solutions, gains credibility from the approval authority.

Applying It To The Corners

For the Strengths, Weaknesses and Threats portion of this tool's process, you don't have to worry about the *Thinking Into the Corners*™ model.

That changes when you start looking at Opportunities, since these must stay within the box limits, even if those limits have been expanded. You must also ensure the filters don't impede ideas, creativity and solutions during the group process.

Quadrant Assessment

When you are faced with several options, a quadrant assessment is another tool you can use to help you decide which action to take. It can also help you prioritize the options based on important characteristics.

In this quadrant diagram, the x axis represents the level of effort from low on the left to high on the right. The y axis represents value, from low on the bottom to high on the top. If your characteristics have a more graduated range, you can further subdivide each quadrant into quadrants and position your options within each quadrant relative to each other to further refine the assessment.

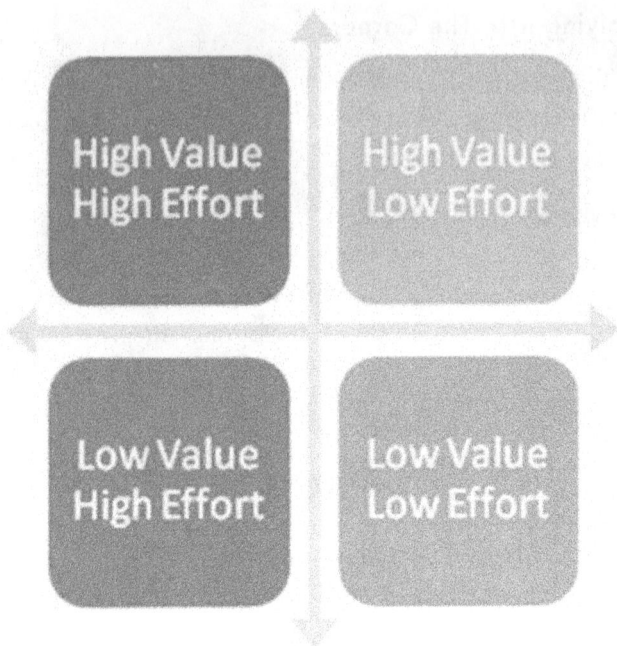

After assessing your various options or solutions, the ones that end up in the top right quadrant are the most likely to implement first since they give you a high value with a low effort. It doesn't mean you wouldn't also implement something with a low value and low effort. The technique does ensure you base your decision on solid information.

While there may be more than just value and effort as important characteristics of the options, including cost or risk, for instance, you can start with whichever characteristics you feel are most important and then take the most likely options from the first quadrant assessment. By working them through again with different characteristics, you can move towards the best possible ones options.

Applying It To The Corners

This assessment technique usually used after you have stretched into the corners and found initiatives or solutions to implement. While you should have already considered your box limits by the time you get to this stage, you should still keep them in mind as you assess the solutions or initiatives, just in case something slipped by.

You also need to monitor the filters when you or the team assign value and effort to the ideas. Since ideas in a quadrant can be influenced by negative filters, this could impact your ability to choose which ideas are best to move forward with.

Quick Summary

Key Points

➡ Traditional tools can still be used to generate ideas "Into the Corners."

➡ It's how you and the team think about limits when generating ideas that makes the difference.

➡ Sometimes, you need to adapt the tools slightly to make them work better.

Executive Tips

➡ Idea-generating tools are just that, tools. They are simply a means to get people to think.

➡ Get someone else to facilitate sessions so you can fully participate and won't inadvertently influence the process.

Traps to Avoid

➡ Falling into the same approach once you start using the tools.

➡ Forgetting to come back to the box limits to maintain a boundary around ideas.

➡ Letting circle limits, including certain personality traits, influence the process.

Your Plan

Based on what you've read, what will you do to develop creative ideas and solutions to improve results?

What are you going to do?	When

Notes

Index

About the Author

Michel Theriault is Founder of *Success Fuel for Managers*, a training & consulting firm providing strategic and management support that helps managers assess, analyze, develop and implement initiatives to get better results.

Other books by the Author

Quick Guides for Managers (Series)
Write to Influence, 2012

Win More Business - Write Better Proposals
Published March, 2010

Managing Facilities & Real Estate
Published December 2010

Contact Information

Please feel free to connect with the Author.

Blog: www.successfuelformanagers.com

Twitter: www.twitter.com/micheltheriault

LinkedIn: www.linkedin.com/in/micheltheriault

E-mail: michel@successfuelformanagers.com